Author biography

Cornelius B. McCoy is a Technology, Motivation, Researcher, and Educational Enthusiast in addition to being a lifelong learner. Cornelius started his journey in technology and blockchain when wax.io airdropped him his 1st of 5 Street Fighter NFTs sometime in the first few months of the year 2021. After discovering this broad new world of possibilities (Web3).

This led to an interest in all things tech and tech business-related. Cornelius is Dedicated to being the allocator and facilitator of the proper mindset, resources, & intel to assist you in the construction of your Learning & Enterprise goals. Admittedly not a legal, tax, or financial professional but an inquisitive builder as he puts it. Invites you on this journey of

discovery, building, learning, growth, & success.

For Questions or Inquiries
Contact: bluemountaintech@zohomail.com or
bluemountaintech@protonmail.com

An Immersive Introduction into Blockchain & Business

An Unfair Advantage For the Innovators of Tomorrow. Leverage Your Perspective by Knowing a Great Founder Is A Learner and A Leaner Can Always Be A Great Leader..

Cornelius B. McCoy

ISBN 978-93-5610-212-5

Published in India 2022 by Pencil

A brand of
One Point Six Technologies Pvt. Ltd.
123, Building J2, Shram Seva Premises,
Wadala Truck Terminal, Wadala (E)
Mumbai 400037, Maharashtra, INDIA
E connect@thepencilapp.com
W www.thepencilapp.com

CONTENTS

Preface

This book is meant to immerse the growing mind into a state of learning and construction of the future. With this book, you will be armed with the perspective to go forth and bring

about new opportunities for yourself and for those around you. This book is made to bring your interest in technology & business to the surface so that you act on them with confidence.

Ask youself what if my money were technology instead of having a flying paper plane as your favorite toy. Having a millennium falcon that actually flies, that's what Crypto, Blockchain, Decentralization, Tokenization, NFTs, and so on are doing to these paper fiat notes that we have grown so accustomed to. While the paper notes keep printing and printing most people have only heard of Bitcoin possibly Etherium and Dogecoin going unbeknownst to those people there are literally thousands of crypto all of them being Technologies. Not all of them however are currencies.

All investments should be scrutinized with the most analytical eyes some of these Technologies are useless and we'll only have value until the world finds out that they don't and that window of time many crypto traders, stakers & yield farmers take advantage of. Some of these startup crypto projects are scams just like anything else and take millions and billions of dollars. That's why it's important to be familiar with technology and science not just from an investment standpoint but from an engineering perspective. Technology is being extended out of our mental capability so we should familiarize ourselves with not just the user aspects but the creator aspects as well. In today's age insurance contracts, art, and music among other things can be sealed in digital mechanisms call NFTs that can occur interest in value.

Until now banks have had all the computational know-how, now everyone with the internet can access crypto in some cases for free. Painters photographers graphic designers and many more can be signed sealed and delivered digital ownership of assets that can gain value forever and be transferred from one platform or game to another. The price of any crypto means nothing just as the price of any liability means nothing because it's a liability you must learn enough to interact with these Technologies around you so that you have only assets one might tell you to invest long-term before trading options and one might tell you vice versa the important thing is to steady and increasingly do both or do one and constantly improve it creations of thought only to energy Aida mind include inventions images used in Commerce symbols artistic and literary work if you ask the WIPO or the world intellectual property organization intellectual property can be separated into three categories trademarks patents and copyrights the blockchain among other things will give the artist power over both the record label and the pirate. This book is about recognizing the opportunities of the newer future and positioning yourself to capitalize on these great upward trends.

Disclaimer*

Information contained in this book is for informational/entertainment purposes only and should not be considered a source of advice or credit analysis with respect to the material presented. The information and/or documents within this book do not constitute legal or financial advice. They should never be used without seeking the advice of a financial professional to determine how best to meet your particular needs.

Neither the publisher nor the author guarantee nor otherwise promises any results that may be obtained by using the content of this book. You should never invest without first consulting an advisor and conducting your own research and due diligence. To the fullest extent permitted by law, the publisher and the author disclaim any and all liability in the event any contents, commentary, analysis, opinions, advice, and/or recommendations contained in this book prove to be inaccurate, incomplete or unreliable or result in any investment or other losses. The content contained or made available by way of this book is not intended to and does not constitute nor substitute for legal advice or investment advice. No attorney-client relationship is formed. The publisher and the author are providing this book and its contents on an "as is" basis. Your use of the information in this book is at your own risk.

Acknowledgements

First, I would like to thank the Lord God for the perspective to see the opportunity for growth first within myself and then in the world around me. I would then thank my dear mother for nurturing my cunning soul in the times
it required it most, for encouraging me to always aim high while thinking outside of the box. I'd like to thank the Hampton Roads Area for being a hub for innovators, trendsetters, and overall genius-level creators.
I'd like to thank my family for being the source of inspiration and realization in my life. Last but not least I thank you the reader for the mind to take an alternative perspective and additional tools. To leverage your future interactions
for your highest good, with the ever-changing & evolving world around us.

1. Intro - The R&D Approach

Information contained in this book is for informational purposes only and should not be considered a source of advice or credit analysis with respect to the material presented. The information and/or documents within this book do not constitute legal or financial advice. They should never be used without seeking the advice of a financial professional to determine how best to meet your particular needs.

Neither the publisher nor the author guarantee nor otherwise promises any results that may be obtained by using the content of this book. You should never invest without first consulting an advisor and conducting your own research and due diligence. To the fullest extent permitted by law, the publisher and the author disclaim any and all liability in the event any contents, commentary, analysis, opinions, advice, and/or recommendations contained in this book prove to be inaccurate, incomplete or unreliable or result in any investment or other losses. The content contained or made available by way of this book is not intended to and does not constitute nor substitute for legal advice or investment advice. No attorney-client relationship is formed. The publisher and the author are providing this book and its contents on an "as is" basis. Your use of the information in this book is at your own risk.

This book is a recognition of the potential in web3/blockchain and technology as well as a toolset of reference, a basis on which to immerse your learning from the outside looking in. In preparation for a new career, launching a business, or marketing campaign. This book is made to inspire & aid the facilitation of start-up studios, incubators, accelerators, and overall innovation toward a renewable energy-efficient world. Firstly decide that you will participate in these industries in some sort of way because your skill and your future are directly linked if not one and the same. Secondly, take a basic course (Free or Paid) in blockchain/web3 or some field of technology. In every field, you can find free resources and learning platforms to begin your journey in that new direction. Whether it's renewable energy, blockchain, cybersecurity, or something else.

Free certifications can take one further than they might expect coupled with problem-solving skills and a great attitude. In Technology and learning alike it can be your attitude toward problem-solving that blasts you past the competition. Thirdly, it is imperative that you pick a major in one of these fields so that if you are in the job market you can make top dollar. Would you like to focus on accounting software for renewable energy? Possibly a smart contract auditor? You may solely focus on blockchain stocks and assets or only want to design the front ends of blockchain websites. Maybe you want to master Linux operating system or make hardware products in the home decor space. No matter what it is hone in and master that aspect of disruptive technology and you position yourself at the top. The early adopters will be greatly rewarded for jumping in with courage and leading in these industries. Those who refuse to learn will undoubtedly be left behind. There will be an estimated 75 billion devices connected to the net by 2025. With all those connected and becoming all the more, intelligent humans will undoubtedly become more intelligent.

Fifth start networking with others already in the space and those entering the space. Networking in the blockchain industry will boost your potential to find a job, co-founder, or employee. It said that by 2025 10% of all GDP (gross domestic product) for the world is expected to be on the blockchain. The GDP as of 2022 is 95 Trillion dollars. So as of now by 2025, there will be 9.5 Trillion dollars on the blockchain. With these technologies being so new there is a massive opportunity for ownership at every level. With the advent of blockchain, NFTs AI, Quantum Computing, Crypto, Crypto Mining, and various other industries. These technologies are not only disrupting and changing other industries but creating entire other sub-industries that are not seen by the non-technical naked eye. Sort of like when automobiles and electricity were created, they started various other industries that did not exist before. That is the time we are in right now. Prof. Klaus Schwab founder and executive chairmen of THe World Economic Forum coin the phrase "4th industrial revolution." The Forth industrial revolution will be spurred by the fusion of multiple technologies

- Machine Intelliegnece

- Gene Editing

- Nano Technology

- Smart Material

- Robotics

- 3-D Printing

- Blockchain

- Big Data

- Quantum Computing

This Book is made for a team of at least 2 people. For best use as a research, development, and reference point for your coming success. These questions and statements should be answered by you in the form of success as well as innovation. Use the resources in this book. Contact us by email if necessary to learn more about how some of the tools can better assist you in your research & development journey. The intel in this document is broken up into lists of execution and solution to your passive income opportunity and research and development growth. The success of the research & development comes because what you learn cannot be taken away and can always be utilized in the future for creation and innovation. When you take a course or get coaching make sure it's well worth the cost and that they are truly helping you. In reality, you could contact a few friends and make a game out of this tool to bring hyper-growth & speed to your operations. Get educated through easy free research, free resources, & courses. As a beginner though it's good to start with the free stuff. Don't buy your way into research & development. Create your own research and development, that puts you automatically in the front. By learning new skills, collaborating, & creating through research you can do the same thing as the latest "guru" and most likely way more legitimate.

Real entrepreneurs provide value & service before asking for money. Rasmus Koss Hartmann Copenhagen Business School wrote the paper, Towards an Entrepreneurial Economy? The Entrepreneurship Industry and the Rise of the Veblenian Entrepreneur. With blazing fingers pointed at the newly termed "Wantrprenuer" industry. This is the perspective that people are selling the lifestyle of business success & entrepreneurship while not actually being successful at business just successful at making you think so. More for social perspective & fancy lifestyle at your expense than actual productivity & innovation. Persist in research, not failure. Take advice with a grain of salt as you learn the technologies, processes, & systems for yourself. Separate yourself by knowing & finding out rather than ending up out of your money, time, and feeling like you know less than you did before. In other words, skip directly over the wannabes. A key question to ask yourself as a value-driven researcher is how can a small business impact various industries in ways that large companies cannot? Those gaps are underserved markets that you can attack with value to drive innovation and the world economy. In the 1st section of this document, the statements will be split up by you and your team and treated as questions. Questions to be answered in your assembling most leveraged aid in your Business, Technology Company, R&D, General Learnership, ETC. Albeit a roadmap is frequently mistaken and considered a static report or — something recorded once and afterward left pretty much finished. —truly a guide is a living, powerful archive. Your plans will change, your customers will change and your processes and systems will undoubtedly change.

Use Vibrant colors on your visual Roadmap!! In light of this, track down ways of having your roadmap incorporate your thinking behind every one of the topics, stories, themes, and perspectives you've decided to incorporate. Your group, investors, and anybody you've given admittance to see the roadmap ought to have the opportunity to know why these things are taking place. Advancement/Development of your organization's roadmap will be a liquid interaction, liable to changes whenever from your organization or the market. Therefore, you really want to think about your roadmap as a living visual archive and or documentation to realize the reason why you've decided to focus on it. Knowing the value of your content & research to your audience makes it easier to monetize and by others getting a view into your roadmap understanding & prospectus, you will have an instant edge in content analytics which is paramount in the customer-facing aspects of your technologies and organizations.

When researching, interacting with, and or doping a demo of different systems, protocols, processes, and tools. Even if you are not into technology try to look at these platforms and tools to aid your forward strategies. Many Founders today are non-technical. Even in being that one must continue to learn as much technology as one possibly can. It is important to understand these things from your perspective as best you can by keeping a growing ever-increasing understanding of said matters. So essentially we are moving into a new phase of the internet and technology as a whole. Business Communication, what does it mean to your group, company, or organization if anything? It should mean some sort of research & development outside of just randomly surfing the internet. Every business no matter how small should have some resources and/or time allocated to R&D or some sort of start-up process. Constantly building on your database while learning to build upon both old & new products & services.

Finding the information is the 1st step and the easiest step. It's the allocation of this proper reuse of this information to monetize it that will take the most focus. This sometimes can be a daunting task for the individual but easier in a group. Optimized group thinking is an essential part of whatever R&D process you set in place. The information must be gathered, sorted, and turned into monetary gain. This can often have different moving parts that must be moving simultaneously to get the desired outcome. With a few computers, printers, projectors, & whiteboards you now have your own Startup incubator/R&D department whatever you can become to drive innovation in your own business and in any industry you choose. Whether it's a business incubator for your area or again just your own R&D department it's essential for you and your company to be involved in learning & innovation. Your group, business, or organization could very well be responsible for discovering new methodologies and technologies in the near future. In this day and age, the individual can do things like lend money and get 18 percent APY on that money. 40 years ago it was near impossible to be your own bank and lend money and receive massive interest like the banks themselves. Today there are literally lend, stake, and yield farm money, from money that you invested once.

This is a significant shift in economic energy and momentum. With interest generated from these cryptographic mathematical equations in combination with open source technology and various other mechanisms. It's now possible for individuals or small groups to impact certain sectors of the industry just like a corporation and sometimes much better. Groups in 2022 are extracting value from various platforms in an organized way to allocate those acquired digital assets to leverage for further revenue, acquisitions, and inventions. Did you know that many projects use platforms like Github & Openzepplin to literally take existing crypto projects, put their own spin on them and release it as their own company? This is a part of creating, applying & adapting to the current landscape of technology. It happens every day and will continue to as we must continue to build on ideas that are already working while creating completely new things simultaneously. The idea is to bring the best and freshest. Income rationale, revenue logic, and capital allocation should correspond to current and future best processes in business and innovation. An examination and improvement or R&D organization that finds the most recent innovations in many technological sectors and makes an interpretation of those discoveries into various digital & physical formats devices structures and configurations to drive income to additionally influence and capture both computerized and genuine resources through research & development.

Such an office will deliver imaginative groundbreaking thoughts, creative plans, and income-producing items, strategies, products & services. Research and development divisions themselves don't need to be huge or costly; they require diligent and imaginative leadership. Innovative thoughts can emerge out of any individual from a group, from the most junior to the most senior. While all things considered, those with the most progressive logical and technological thoughts are probably going to come from science or geek foundations, it's essential to perceive that plenitude of capabilities doesn't consequently make somebody more innovative. A creative nature can frequently be just down to character and experience, which is the reason having a diverse R&D division is significant. Pioneers will generally savor the opportunity to test, stretch boundaries, pose inquiries and consider some fresh possibilities. Variety itself can mean having a combination of ages, abilities, experience, foundations, and identities. It's the best method for keeping thoughts streaming and having a scope of various perspectives. Characterized clear definitive objectives and goals in R&D with measurements set up so the achievement is quantifiable&/or measurable. In a matter of finance and crypto especially keep CFPB.gov in your toolkit. The Consumer Finance Protection Bureau has mechanisms to protect you and your organization against fraudulent activities. Free resources are an essential part of any research incubator. An engineer's mindset toward innovation deploys all resources toward focus new achievements technologies and inventions. Large technology companies facilitate an idea-fueled environment (R&D) to constantly invent the latest technologies.

This has translated to Open source and or community-driven R&D efforts from both the tech giants and the up and coming tech enthusiasts of the space. In business and technology companies and individuals are often slow to adapt to bring in new creative processes even if the old ones are not working. Execute the old whilst generating the new, Bringing on NEw products must be implemented from the smallest business with a pen & pad to an enterprise IT infrastructure company. If you're going to always invent then you must take the Bezos coined "Always Day One". The Flagship product must be maintained yes only while inventing the extension of that product or service that will most likely be used internally. Which will make its way to decision-makers within a company or investment pool and be monetized externally. Often the masses complain about tech giants while not presenting alternatives to the space. On The flip side of that clothes invest billions into clear scams that had no legitimacy from the get-go or failed projects that were simply bad ideas or just plain didn't work. Through community-driven networks like blockchain communities, these aspects can be governed by internal research and monetization. Inventing multiple technologies for internal-facing monetization use cases and then deploying those mechanisms that already generate revenue internally. This brings ideas to judgment quickly because they already working internally.

So instead of investing billions in ideas that "might work". Start a start-up team or R&D department for free with community-based research and incentives to construct multiple forward and inward-facing business plans, monetization strategies/methods, inventions, and technologies. The book A Lean Start-Up pulls these ideas into a focused spectrum To bring your products to monetization ASAP. Bring simplicity to the invention by letting everyone invent. Prioritizing and monetizing those inventions. With quickly making you MVP. Minimal viable products from centering your company around research and development. Your company revolves around. How did tech founders get their products and ideas out there? Identify parts of your business that has a multiplying and compounding effect on your business. There must be growth equations and or success algorithms to ensure success. Skill abilities and connections are the main 3 components in finding co-founders for your business or businesses. Skills that are fundamental to your success must be found in your co-founders. There must also be continuous learning and documentation of this learning to be translated income various formats for various cases such as media, consulting, and invention.

2.. Blockchain and Incubation

Always have qualified professionals about the specifics of your blockchain business. Keep aware of IRS notices, also inferring/can we use that exchange whats the actual tax treatment do we disclose earnings as we trade-off when we convert to fiat? Don't be in a position where you raise millions and the value of your portfolio drops because of claiming your project is a utility token and you are not. Securities tokens are more like shares of a company or a stock while a Utility token is used for goods and services within an ecosystem. The HOWE TEST is the metric to decide if the coin is a Utility or Security.BE sure to have handy Tax Professionals & Attornies for every step of the way. More specifically and ideally focused solely on securities and/or digital assets. Your company can have REG CF securities crowdfunding up to 1.1 million dollars is pre-sale and still, be ok under securities law. Once you go up REG C, B, A+ it gets very specific on who you can and can't sell to. If you go up in Reg then you have to start dealing with accredited investors and or other similar higher-level investors.

That moves away from the open access to everyone which is what crypto is in one main part about. So will you associate your cost with Bootstrap for the 1st 6 months to get a prototype up so we can classy as a utility or should you go find funding to become a security token to pursue traditional investors? There are no taxes due on the equity raise of securities tokens. Tho this process will take more funds upfront. On utility tokens in some states, you must pay income taxes for software as a service. When consulting with your team of Tax & Legal professionals know the right questions to ask, find Tax Advantages and Structures, and remember you cant have convertible notes with sole member LLC income structures, a Delaware C-Corp is most ideal. That being a security token project.

You must designate the right questions for your specific project and professionals. Rules and regulations for shareholders of your company can they be other LLCs or entities? Can they be in the US or worldwide? Setting up business entities for projects and startups' best practices. If you're going to be a utility token it might make more sense to be a US entity just make sure you're a true utility token. Securities are often based in other countries for tax advantages and incentives. Keep a paper trail document everything you can for would-be investors.

Start with a business plan then document everything there thereafter including why certain decisions were made. Don't pay an attorney or tax person to do your business plan. Have attorneys tweak your business plan, Are you interested in Law firms that are qualified to help with ICOs, NFT, securities, and tokenized assets. What're their qualifications for knowing cryptocurrency taxation or regulation? You looking for someone and or individuals nuanced in your specific situation. Build a solid team for your project - Key Players. Tax Pro, Securities law Attorney, ICO STO Attorney, or COO - to Help push things through for advisors and communicate thoroughly, and last but not least your CEO. What's just compensation- no one wants to get paid in only tokens. X numbers in dollars in cash for a retainer and the rest in tokens perhaps? When receiving tokens from a project using the 83 b election vesting schedule to pay taxes to be paid on those tokens at their initial receiving.

Blockchain firms can raise funds through traditional means such as friends and family, venture capitalists, and other institutional investors, or through a "public" offering such as a Security Token Offering (STO) or an Initial Coin Offering (ICO) (ICO). However, in this context, "public" is a relative term. It can mean that anybody can participate (in the case of ICOs) or that only accredited investors can participate (in the case of most STOs).

So that if/once the tokens go up in value you won't pay those high taxes and get to pay taxes on the amount they were worth initially to keep the bulk of your profit. The recent Web3/Blockchain emergence is much like the emergence of the internet in the late '90s. Blockchain will be just as impactful if not even more. NFTs will consume whole industries and crypto is seeking to give you the same power as your bank. Web 2 was about information while Web3 is about sharing value. New crypto start-ups are being built on decentralized protocols. A crypto start-up is any start-up that is going to use crypto to Raise money, gain customers, or expand internationally. to build a worldwide audience. In traditional start-ups, these are the 3 main reasons they usually fail but with the advent of crypto, these things can be solved early in the start-up process. Crypto has great solutions for each of these problems. It can be hard for someone outside of silicon valley or without a rich friend to raise money for a business.

Crypto fundraising helps solve these problems by making your ideas more accessible to people who will believe in your idea in a slightly new industry. Lots of start-ups suffer from the cold start problem when launching they often don't have any initial customers. Crypto helps with this because projects can give small pieces of ownership to early customers for supporting their network. Tech companies most of the time piggyback off of other networks to gain customers but by giving customers ownership some crypto start-ups are building great early eco-systems on their own. Crypto allows for a worldwide user base from day one. This helps you navigate and avoid costly and challenging payment integrations one country at a time. Local regulations and bank accounts in each country would be very challenging to set up one at a time. Crypto is the ultimate answer for global start-up expansion from day one.

When starting your company in the blockchain industry ask yourself what problem are you trying to solve. How are you going to use blockchain and does it need to be on the blockchain to be solved.
What do you hope to accomplish with this technology from an inward standpoint to a customer-facing perspective? Some are looking for greater speed in

transactions with it being possible to move 100 million dollars at the same speed it would move 1 dollar. Some are looking for entirely new revenue sources like yield farming, flash loans, Exchanges, mining, and many more sub-niches. Some Are looking toward security and lower-cost benefits. That could be great for a start-up that is bootstrapped for cash. In most cases, from a customer-facing standpoint, they do not give a darn bout the features of your products and all the bells and whistles. All they care about is the benefit and what that does for them so lead with that and that alone every single time. Drive the benefits of your product home, not the features that you spent 357 hours coding or overseeing the development of. As hard as your work the customer doesn't care about that they want the benefit of the product and the benefit only

Companies and governments around the world want to start incubators, accelerators workshops, innovation studios, venture builders, etc. However, it can be a lot to think about and difficult to get going. Most of the most successful programs have been started by students, small groups/ individuals, and not the big executives. It's simple, business incubators remodel thoughts into operating organizations.

It's a supply-and-take relationship in which: The organization offers its early business unit the support and guidance it desires to become a commercial enterprise

The incubator acts as a catalyst for the organization to turbocharge innovation and develops a pipeline of successful new ventures

What are your theories around business and entrepreneurship? More innovative ideas or traditional ideas?

Will you choose disruptive progressive ideas over conventional commercial enterprise ideas?
Will you have a focus on the new generation and throughout what sectors and why? In what ways can you facilitate the help of legal and IP services to keep pressure off of your founding teams or business incubation/accelerator scenarios. Constantly take into account it's your role to help them accomplish in 4 months what would otherwise take a year and a half.

Proximity, industry literacy, and strength of network are key in any incubation/accelerator in today's age. 1st always clarify your goals and what you trying to achieve with each venture (note this may change as the planning and products progress) but one must be clear at the outset of each venture to plan the proper approach and resources. Proximity, industry literacy, and strength of network are key. It's about forcing your will for invention and innovation into a tangible business and or utility format in multiple directions at once. What role what you like as a Founder, CEO, or CFO, or would you just like to remain in the incubator setting to constantly invent. The shared vision of the future brings about great infrastructure for creation. Lowering the risk of investment a solid founding team of a core studio can work side by side with VCs and employees for years to come making a better cohesive unit to deploy IP in a rapid fashion. It is paramount that a core team be productive through thick and thin agreement and disagreement. Will you all make up the ideas in-house or bring ideas from outside entrepreneurs. Your team should be working on multiple projects at once but not every single project in the studio.

Disruptive innovation & invention through industry and citizen science alike need not wait and is never waiting. Constant learning and facilitation of these learnings and resources into an agile, highly profitable, and innovative MVP is the initial goal. So that's may drive you to get more funding, get acquired, or, expand the business. You have to have a great theory to look into the future its what I refer to as a High Base Level Overview where you can are collecting all of this information at once while honing in on an individual or chosen sectors of interest. For example, google 20 percent protects culture which states that anyone that works at Google has the opportunity to work on side projects. This type of culture drives employees' engagement in business communication, innovation, collaboration, incubation, and disruption. This is the type of setting you will be fostering so that your ideas nay flourish into tangible service and infrastructure. At one time Gmail itself was a 20% project at Google and now it's the most used email in the world. With that being said there must never be a failure to launch an initial product or MVP. With your MVP never take more than one month to build.

Any products and services that are still being bought about should fall under a strong IP strategy. Books like Always

Day One prepare you and The Lean Start-Up Focus on constant building and iteration to achieve multiple developments at once.

Gain real-time proof of demand by building something that either solves a problem or earns people money. Plain and simple, take the learning path of you and your studio team directly to the top. Ideate, iterate, test, get profitable, fund, find founders, developers, etc. Then moving on to the next project is my best advice and perspective if you wish you invent and innovate. Don't get caught up in owning and running the business that business because you are an inventor and facilitator and you have more of that to do. It's simple, business incubators remodel thoughts into operating organizations. It's a supply-and-take relationship in which: The organization offers its early business unit the support guidance it desires to become a commercial enterprise. The incubator acts as a catalyst for the organization to turbocharge innovation and develops a pipeline of successful new ventures

3. Validate From All Angles

Put everyone to work because sometimes experts don't know diddly. When selecting Advisors and Experts that's not a cure-all. Put their behinds to work, admit that they or you don't know anything instead admit to the winds of change learn, and build. Never let the most tried and true experts stop your co-creation in learning, advancement, & technological prowess. Even the best of experts we're wrong at some point in a big way.

Microsoft Ceo said about the iPhone "It doesn't appeal to customers because business owners won't pay $500 for a phone with no keyboard." Then tossing it off with a laugh, Thomas Watson of IBM in 1943 said there would be a market for about 5 computers around the world. Experts know the past, not the future.

That's where you come in to take responsibility and ownership of innovation from your future tense perspective.
Go from why not to having it built and functional. Be the definition of a facilitator. When you google if being a facilitator
it says: "A facilitator plans, guides, and manages a group event log to meet its goals.

To facilitate effectively, you must be objective and focus on the "group process." That is, the ways that groups work together to perform tasks, make decisions, and solve problems."

\Whetaher you are well versed in web or blockchain development or not you should be well versed in research methods, methodologies tactics, and, tools.

To start your invention and research journey you will want to immerse yourself in your chosen field by categorizing

- Industry news

- Industry magazines

- Government websites

- Scholarly texts

- Academic books

- Encyclopedias

- Respected websites

- Interviews with experts

- Pdfs

- Blogs

- Newsletters

- Videos

- Courses

- Certifications

You are constantly hyper leaner, microlearning, and incremental learning. You are the generator, the engine to either directly
build or facilitate the direct or indirect building and learning of everything around. You are the at service of the world as an immersive learner
who leverages the latest intelligence and ideas into tangible products and systems.
In a start-up, there is always the element of risk so you must learn, facilitate, and co-create across the board. I can't stress enough once products are established you should have a lot of
time to hone in on a few things and perfect them. your thirst for learning and working on new ideas must wait
because honing in on those few things of the product will keep you ahead of the competition and your customers happy. Customer success comes from a fluent understanding or
Visual Design and Interaction design/UX design. Interaction design/UX is how the product works and Visual design is how it looks.
As far as different aspects of the Overview and potential hyper-focus for success you have:

- Engineering

- Product

- Design

- Sales

- Marketing

- Finance

- Leadership

- Management

When building & releasing products have a constant feedback loop. The people that wait in line for the new PS5,iPhone, & use the latest software, etc. You should be talking to them and gathering as much feedback about the product as possible because that will translate into improved product design and features. When speaking with them about validated problems. pain points & validate solutions. Don't change your product every single piece of feedback. What about business or tells you that they adopt technology early. Build a list of early adopters to set in motion feedback loops. "ASK FOR ADVICE ABOUT EVERYTHING." That's one of your most important jobs. Start the conversation. You are not required to be an expert today in any field today to become a million or billionaire tomorrow (figuratively speaking).

You do however have to begin to learn development and engineering

as well as aspects of finance. You are an instrument of learning, building, and facilitation innovation. At the highest level, you understand that material technologies are driven by both social consensuses

as well as overall evolution. You are in a hyper transition of Facilitation-Learning (Base level Overview) & Development/Learning (Honing/Focused) on specific features for new & existing products.

When hiring developers it is important to run some sort of test project. You're looking for how they act, how they communicate, and how they solve problems. Do they just return with a finished product?

Did they show you the early stages of it and clear up any issues or hurdles. That's what your looking for find some user/development advisor mentors to help you filter out talent.

When hiring Advisors don't pay for introductions and don't give away your entire business. When seeking advice in any area first seek free counsel then professional council then legal counsel.

The benefits of having an advisory board are a built-in network, resources, and fast decision-making. Once a year send your advisors a strategy deck. Showing high-level aspects and what you look to accomplish over the next year,

Along with this ask them to do some work. Maybe an introduction, help with outsourcing or get on a sales call.

Always start with free consultations, Professionals, and

lastly Attorneys. Each will better equip you to better communicate and navigate your interaction with the next. Ultimately lead to the results you're looking for. Identify gaps in your knowledge then seek out council & intel that will fill those gaps. ideally, they will be 3- 5 years ahead of you. Their experiences will be relevant because the timeline is close. Have a broad set of advisors but know you can outsource all decision-making instead of incorporating all their advice/stories/verbal case studies into your overall perspective. In compensation for advisory possibly look to a start-up advisor option grant of around a 1/4 of a percent to 3/4 of a percent vesting monthly over 2 years in most cases if they are helping you over the long hall. You yourself must get familiar with what TECH STACKS the most successful start-ups & companies are currently using. Development tech stacks contain

-
  Programming language

- Database

- Framework

- Server

If you have a technical friend ask what tech stack you should use ask all the questions you can.
Build the MVP of the MVP or build a MEVO of A MEVO i.e test test test!!! Build the minimum features and make them great.

Outline 2 features that it does today and connect that to your grand vision. Start learning how to build blockchain projects, clickable projects, no-code solutions that came be improved upon as you learn

Things that in a short time will become functional to the point of revenue generation. Depending on the level of interaction, integrations, scalability, and data sources among

other things some tools will be better than others. If you don't know what it takes to build what's in your mind

some developers will throw anything together and call it magnetic while taking you for a loop.

Developers believe they can build anything but you are the wiser when you know what it takes.

If your app or website is of service across the world it would behoove you that your site reliability team or remote developers are scheduled at opposite hours like in the AM hours. For the mental stability of your local team and overall business. Ask developers for 2 "Agile Theories" on how to maintain software and systems in the future. Hire Intelligence, resourcefulness, & kindness, not resumes and experience. In development, at times experience can

be outdated and supplemented by sheer Intelligence. Can their past experience amalgamate with company intentions to bring about desired workflow and results? Communication is kept in every direction pushing introverts to ask questions and extroverts to hone in. Pick awesome people Matt Decoursey of Fullscale.io puts it "Dude if you drop a term in the punch bowl the punch doesn't taste good anymore." Don't let bad apples into the cider. You want people who will be agile unwavering problem solvers who can be hyper-introverted but speak up when things need to be said or don't make sense. Code tests and interviews aside you won't know until it's time to work. That's why you want an unwavering learner and problem solver to be on the task.

- What makes you happy?

- What are your life & professional goals?

- What professional areas do you need to improve?

- Why are you considering leaving your current job?

- What have you liked about your past or current employers?

- Do you like working alone or with a team more?

- Do you want a leadership role or a task-focused position?

- Do you prefer front-end or back-end development?

- What are your best skills and abilities as a developer?

- What about web development do you least like doing?

- Are you usually on time?

- What are you looking for in an employer?

- What's your greatest strength

- What's your greatest strength as a developer?

Hiring affects you, the employee, the company, the culture, the environment, & product itself. Competence and courteously over the hotshot genius who nobody likes.

When your selecting for a specific task the candidate doesn't have to be good at everything but must be excellent at that specific task in more broad roles seek out the well rounded. Hire people smarter and better than yourself at times that's why you are smart. You don't have to be the smartest if you select the right people though and still achieve just as great results. There is never a final version of software or technology. Your business must make sure that it is clear that your business makes clear that the code produced will have copyrights & IP owned by you and your organization. Organizations have to maintain and improve this software forever, thus an agile IP strategy must be in place for such rapid changes.

For example, the Cleveland Indians when switching their Branding to the guardians planned and put millions into a rebranding soon after the role out they found out about a nearby roller skating team with the same. There most likely will be some sort of profit-sharing agreement because their

IP strategy wasn't in place or didn't do a full screening before the rebranding roll-out.

Once you establish a product or company and go from quote end quote 0 to 1 Your company will be worth the net present value of all future cash flows so

prudent decisions must be made now.

So 1stly you must be immersing yourself in the learning of aspects of finance & engineering while honing in on current product features.

Perter Theil states that you "create X amount of value and capture Y% of X." Learn or make something valuable than capture a portion of that value.

When it comes to product Dan Martell is noted for saying the P in MVP stand for "a whole lot of work. He suggests instead a "MEVO" a Minimum Viable Equiable Offer

This states that you don't have to build the product to validate the product. Instead, validate the simulation. Marketing site with sales page, one-page website, possibly a screenshot of the soon to be the product he states it just has to be interesting enough to buy at that level so that the next level can be built.

We see this in the case of the SchollyMe app that helps facilitate athletes' recruitment on an international level. More specifically they started this venture using a very similar approach to the MEVO approach.

In which they collected E-mails in person to get early adopters who loved the idea. They had laminated slides and pitch decks to garner investments. After they obtained those funds they went on to build multiple platforms now valued in the hundred million if not billions. They saw a market need for athletic recruiting mechanisms in China and developed the concept of a recruiting/sports-based social platform. So by being resourceful and conceptual they solved a problem for over a billion people. Just By Validation & Communication. Simple steps took place, the 1st was market research or the concept, and the second whats resourcefulness or invention.

Spotting financial and technological & intellectual arbitrage opportunities is your game. Validate only seeing the glass half full, shoot for the moon and have faith in the future as you co-create it. Naveen Jain in an interview with

Tim Bilyeu said when learning a new subject he reads no less than 10 different books and publications on the subject so as to not form a narrow opinion about the future. From a different perspective. Steve Jobs tried to introduce a company uniform apple vest, that the staff did not accept. He then started wearing his well-known black turtle neck. Both of these people (Naveen & Steve) respectively were essentially combining, streamlining, & optimizing their prospective into focused action.

4. Resourcefulness Open-Source

Business Communication what does that mean to your organization of anything, It should mean some sort of R&D outside of randomly searching the internet. Every business no matter

how small should have resources allocated toward R&D or some sort of Start-Up process. Constantly building on your database of knowledge & learning in more optimized ways. Finding

the information isn't the difficult part it's the allocation and reuse of these tools that most people have problems with. The allocation of the proper monetization tools can be difficult for the individual and typically

much easier for a group. Optimized group thinking in a resourceful manner is essentially the start-up process in a nutshell. 3- 4 computers, a few printers, Wi-Fi and you are your own startup, business incubator, or whatever development vessel you may choose. A realm formulating success outside of what your business already knows. Adopting, creating, & applying sign up to give it a whirl again all that valuation data I live right side of my hope to see you their effective techniques for research and development is the future of every business how do you come up with your current decisions? Would it be nice to have an allocated team to gather intel & run tests before your next financial or creative venture? This starts with

coordinated efforts toward expansion and problem-solving. There can be lots of distorted information presented so it is up to us as the examination & development sector to examine then reconstruct these findings to the point of beneficial co-creation. Growth in tech is about refining your current processes & systems while seducing new processes through learning for further expansion. Learning overflows
and can only result in co-creation. Make yourself familiar with the processes and systems of:

- Head Fund Managers

- Corporate Managers

- Financial Analysis

- CPAs

Learn the processes and regulations of these individuals and institutions so you can assist in filling the gaps in your area of the growing market. When large corporations need things created they hire four people just like you with Wi-Fi and internet to sit in a room to search, formulate, test, and develop new ideas/products/services. Surely you can find three willing others once you do you'll have either your

- Business Incubator

- Startup Incubator

- Startup Studio

- Business Accelerator

- Start-Up Accelerator

- Business Development Center

- Research Firm

- Consulting Firm

you must be abreast of the latest in technology compliance and regulation investing in financial literacy and whatever else may I interest you in your business endeavors don't just learn about the tech learn the text itself then learn to delegate after all the autonomous age is a part of now. Let's ask as an investor, how do I find 100% accurate financial statements for any company? ASK THE BEST QUESTIONS!!!!! Don't live in the ethnocentrism of "the business norm." Paul Lemberg's BE UNREASONABLE gives you an insight into and a catalyst to accomplish anything. He states that we already know what to do but let "reasonable thoughts" creep in and stifle our dreams. He tells you to search for the impossible and expect the best. He states to "Grasp the Optimal Scenario" and see it through. This attitude matched with your organization's start-up mentality can & will lead to great success. It's more about the goals & mentality of your organization than individual goals or initial talent. Let your work & organization be greater & outside of yourself so that you can learn from it.

To uphold a value-driven customer experience what else is there to do? The mentality of your organization should be personally invested as well as attentive and this should project through the company's mission & vision. In this day and age learning can and a half years compensate for actually not knowing the technology and help you fast-track or bypass the technology all together with no-code tools, companies, inventions, products, and no code billionaires sprouting up left and right. Films games and other entertainment are now being funded by blockchain technology. Mogul Productions seeks to become the future of film by giving fans sayso in what movies get funded though this is a lofty goal it is worth understanding these Technologies and their implications. Not for what they are in the present but what before what they strive to be in the near and distant future that's the part that you use to leverage to your advantage. So one thing is for certain technology is moving fast but Blockchain, Defi, Crypto, and NFTs will affect every business in the next 2-4 years. So what can you do with the decentralized money markets that are allowing for higher APY than the Traditional Bank APY of 0.03% you want to know how you get 10% to 20% APY consistently.

You want to know what a crypto Ira is and is it tax-free. You want to know how to use a decentralized ledger to ensure future APY. You want a long-term and short-term high-yield strategy with multiple compliant functions. I see or Initial Coin Offerings can be looked at as extremely risky & quick money flips, that's because anyone can create an ICO all these are new technologies but made by who? I suggest you weed out the scamming and low-grade projects immediately. STO (Security Token Offerings are different entirely in my book STOs are for the long-term investment if the technology is good if it is not it would be a short flip like most ICOs after all they may be scams or just bad tech in general, try never to buy cryptocurrency from individuals. If you have to buy from an individual always use a Bitcoin Escrow Service when buying NFTs or crypto from an individual. Also never leave your crypto in an exchange this may result in fraud and Theft only use the exchange for trading or interacting with other protocols what significance within the theory I'm sticking software hold in 10 years for your organization if implemented today cryptographic access to digital assets it would be wise for you to begin acting with these Technologies immediately.

The Start-Up &/or Growth Hacking mentality example is. Linda works at a locally owned grocery store. The owner Dan is having trouble with his computer system and is aware that kinda is tech-savvy.
Linda helps Dan with this and shows him a few tricks to make his CPU run faster. Linda then starts to think about her skills and how they can expand her career. That night she goes home and starts a free course
on cyber security. After a week Linda finds out about open source technology and free tools she can use to solve issues that she learned from her course. Linda then experiments with these tools and realizes that
she can provide multiple services to others with these free tools. Linda after 2 months of learning and putting together her services

asks Dan would he like to partner her tech skills with his network of business owners to provide IT Consultations to other small businesses. Dan agrees and they start a successful consulting firm in less than a month.

Now Linda can no longer work at the grocery store because she is a more valuable asset to herself & to Dan. Now they have achieved a business while spending little to no money.

Open source technology is an awesome thing for a new developer or someone new to break into the game. Open source allows for contribution by anyone who would like to have input. This allows for the best minds from around the world to collaborate in the same place. This means while learning you can work on real-world projects and gain real work skills. Another aspect of Open Source is that it is mostly free to use as a service as well, they make money by providing support and consulting to other businesses. The question being answered now is what happens when Fintech Defi, & Blockchain get open-sourced tools. The answer is new experiments, businesses, money, and opportunities to build. Similar to open-source projects platforms Gitcoin and NEAR University allow people to learn, earn and build in a community setting while learning Blockchain development. With Open Source in the financial realm entrepreneurs in developing countries who know exactly what services the region needs can go to open source libraries and build the product or service. Around 40% of banks use the Cobol coding language. This Language is taught at no top schools and there is a shortage of developers for that language. You then mix that with the advent of new Blockchain, Fintech, Defi, and Open source technology you then have the perfect storm for the massive opportunity. The newer systems are built on newer systems and languages but they will have to interact with these traditional systems.

This is a hypothetical example. However, it is not unrealistic that by the end of the story Linda if had chosen to could have started her own business and/or partnered with someone else.

That's because she constantly added and added to her learning and resourcefulness. 10 years ago to start a software company you had to drive to a computer store to buy physical servers. Then buy software licenses, and write the code for the database. Thousands if not millions of dollars later and many months to 1 year later you could finally start working on the projects that you want to bring to the world.

Now in this age with around $70-$200 you can deploy your own software in 1 day.

With a credit card from anywhere, you can build software infrastructure today. This means that thousands if not millions of

experiments will take place in software, technology itself, and financial services. This happened when Amazon Web Services brought Infrastructure as a service. Years ago if Uber was created in that sluggish era. They would have had to spend millions and wait a long time to test the idea to see if it even worked. If that were the case we most likely would not have uber today. Today anyone can test and deploy software, meaning this same Infrastructure as a service is coming to financial services. With the addition of blockchain, these experiments and new participants will have lots of room for Intellectual as well as financial growth. For example, Doordash provides drives to make deliveries. They also provide financial services to their drivers, this is going to translate to many other industries and some of the growth is going to be brought about by companies and people that are not already in the space.

There are so many opportunities to create new mechanisms for instance a DAO (Decentralized Autonomous Organization) is a Company.
that is completely autonomous and runs itself after you code it one time. This is formed by a collection of Smart Contracts together that form this. This is often used as a governance/voting mechanism
as well as a financial mechanism.

When starting any blockchain project don't worry about decentralization too much at first. Decentralization is sometimes not fully achieved so your job is to take advantage of Decetralizaed
tools for your company and customers optimizing them in a centralized setting. Always always always triplet audit your code. Have code audits extensively before deploying any smart contracts on the blockchain. Blockchain code is mostly unchangeable so you must ensure code audits are thorough before deployment of a Dapp, smart contract, etc. Especially if you will be keeping your customer's funds on-chain. Checking for vulnerabilities is often seen as the most important step before the deployment of any software or online infrastructure.

Crypto currency exchanges are a great source of income, most exchanges are made with a technology called Automated Market Makers which have liquidity pools in the back end

where users are parking their crypto and earning passive rewards for doing so. Trading fees go to the platform but as a developer, you can as some extra profitability by coding it in your smart contracts yourself.

You can code away from the trading fees.

Storing data is a better-done off-chain. When you upload an Image to IFPS (Interplanetary File System) you get a hash where the reference is stored you then put that reference hash

into the smart contract. That's one example of limiting data on-chain. This is important for many blockchains, especially Ethereum. The more data stored on-chain the higher the cost per transaction for everyone.

All of these things are possible because Ethereum took decentralization and added a programmable layer on top of it so that people could develop new things. The blockchain arena is fairly new

and requires an open mind so that you can bring the most value to the space. Using smart contracts built on 1st generation blockchains, however, are facing challenges that are preventing early adoption.

These chains make the smart contract slow to propagate, costly, and do not scale for real-world use-cases. These impediments must be removed before real-world adoption will take place. This is partly the reason for

the up-and-coming release of Ethereum 2.0. When you are

ready to build your software or hardware product don't pay one of those invention firms because you have one good idea. Instead, start a long-term correspondence with multiple professionals to get a well-rounded overview of how to move forward, develop a rock-solid IP strategy, and how to best interact with IP lawyers. Patent Insider is a leading firm in the Intellectual Property Industry. It is vital to have a proper IP strategy in place. No matter if you are making hardware, software, processes, or systems either way it's important. You should be building a full-proof Intellectual Property Strategy with a highly qualified licensed professional.

Cyber Tips

1. Make sure the home network is secure with strong default passwords

2. Log into routers using the web interface

3. WPA2 encryption change WIFI ID

4. Encryption only works with strong passwords

5. Change default Admin names & passwords

6. Enable firewalls

7. Don't use any device without a firewall

8. Free network analysis tools

9. Hide your Wifi

10. DNS cloak

11. Possibly ditch wifi for ethernet cables

12. USB data block Blocker - removes the possibility of data being removed from your device by public USB

13. Webcam cover

14. Dongles instead of using Bluetooth

15. Privacy Screen Protector

16. Ledger & Ledger nano - Hardware/physical crypto wallet

17. SSD or flash drive - external harddrive

18. USB external webcam

19. The art of invisibility & the age of surveillance capitalism

20. A home router that supports firmware - Netgear nighthawk r 7800

21. Raspberry Pie

22. Don't use any device without a firewall

23. Kali Linux- A security auditing system & suit of more than 300 features for your services or platforms security

Resources to get you started

- https://www.scoutely.com/

- https://www.mcgovern.org/

- https://developer.ibm.com/technologies/blockchain/

- web3creators.com/learn-web3

- analyticsindiamag.com/top-10-free-resources-to-learn-blockchain/

- https://www.gartner.com/en/articles/what-is-web3

- https://www.coursera.org/learn/private-equity

- https://app.cadena.dev/dashboard

- https://academy.quantcast.com/trainings

- https://near.org/education/

- https://www.near.university/

- https://www.near.university/earn/ambassador-program

- https://www.nvidia.com/en-us/training/online/

- https://bounties.network/gettingStarted

- https://gogetfunding.com/

- https://digitalcorps.gsa.gov/about

- https://www.dol.gov/general/topic/training

- https://www.grants.gov/web/grants/learn-grants/grant-programs.html

- https://www.itgrants.info/

- https://www.itgovernance.co.uk/set-your-organisation-up-for-success-resources

- https://certikit.com/

- https://www.uscybersecurity.net/free-resources-1/

- https://www.knowbe4.com/free-it-security-tools

5. The Amalgamation of Skill & Opportunity

Always prepare your pitch deck prepare. Whether you use it to raise funding or as a guide to lead your team by way of your vision or both. Always have multiple pitch decks on hand, how much money could you raise how can you better adjust your pitch what pieces of your team are missing? Who is your prime customer who can you get on your board of advisors? The dollar has lost 85% of its value since 1971 when we abandon the gold standard in 2009 we found our first defy monetary growing gold Bitcoin now anyone can send money anywhere so how will this adopt two people who don't consider the internet a viable source of revenue. Pools of tokens lock the smart contracts are then used on platforms where individuals with no money can borrow and pay back while making a little money in between and in some cases a lot of startups and research require resources that may not be apparently available or accessible to the naked eye. Set up a rotation of correspondence with organizations institutions associated companies and associations and individuals alike let him know either what you need to execute your plans what you plan to do what you need from them Etc the point is to be constantly finding figuring measuring analyzing formatting designing a locating and inventing. One resource to help with business advisory is his businessadvising.org or https://www.pacificcommunityventures.org/ this resource fits you with a volunteer advisor and an extra cog in your machine/empire for free. The businessadvising.org boasts over a 25% increase in revenue of businesses fitted with a volunteer advisor.

Other free resources to be utilized are as follows but not limited to:

- Community College Small Business Centers

- Score

- SBA

- Small Business Legal Clinics

- Women business Centers

- Minority business Centers

- Veterans Business Outreach Centers

Once you facilitate the learning pattern in your mind before you facilitated the infrastructure you are intelligent as you see yourself to be. If dedicated to learning first then your systems will grow into better places and functions to provide revenue. Firstly prioritize learning, prioritized learning is your way into a better realm of intelligence, action, and life. Prioritized Learning is self-inflicted responsibility in a constantly changing world learning the latest in your field and fields that interest will force you to create in your field. Learning is not just an intake but an output, if there is a new intake there can only be a new output. Goals lead to a pure and accurate destination for your mental consumption. The growth hacking mentality is one of the highest resourcefulness, lucrative action, and fiscally advantageous activities. This age of technological advancement is an amalgamation of what has been created and what is coming to be co-created by you. Another easy way of consuming lots of information at once is free and paid infographics some other ways for the practitioner in science and learning in the New Age of development is Citizen Science in which regular people interact and develop scientific findings and new technological breakthroughs through community efforts.

Zooniverse & Sci-starter are great resources for information to build on. Have an abundance of sources to become the source of development, engineering, and science wholeheartedly, here are a few starting points you could try at:

- Civic science

- Community science

- Citizen science

Engage with those communities while gaining skills from free as well as paid sources and always strive to make a difference. The point of these Citizen Science programs and Community Science programs is to fill the gaps in spaces between professional research and new discoveries. Stay informed on the latest policy in addition to coming bills & proposed infrastructure. Always try to have your say about policy decisions that may influence scientific policy future technological policy and renewable infrastructure you can do this by way of:

- Public Policy Meetings

- Nonprofits academic Institutions

- Government Institutions

Ask them about city regional, state, & federal resources for programs to conduct citizen science or your business projects. They should give you a list of resources that you could contact to learn more. The Future is bright and with unlimited possibilities for professional as well as citizen research. Someone or a many few reading this very book may very well bring about paramount discoveries in the near coming years that will not only fill the gaps but excel past what we already know.